YOU WILL RECEIVE POWER

DR. MARILYN GOOL

CONQUERORS
PUBLISHING

Charlotte, NC

You Will Receive Power

ISBN #978-0-9971292-2-9
Copyright © 2024 by Marilyn Gool
Victory Christian Center
P.O. Box 240433
Charlotte, NC 28224

Published by Conquerors Publishing Company
7228 Kings Ridge Drive
Charlotte, NC 28217

CONTENTS

HOW IT BEGAN
Chapter 1

On the day of Pentecost (a Jewish holiday) about 2 thousand years ago, Jesus sent the Holy Spirit to the earth. A group of 120 men and women were waiting in an upper room. Jesus told them not to leave the city of Jerusalem until the Holy Spirit came. They were unified and continued to pray.

It was an amazing incident. An unusual sound like a powerful wind filled the room. A sign of fire shaped like tongues sat on each person and they were all filled with the power of the Holy Spirit and began to speak in a language they had never learned. People who observed them when they emerged from the room were puzzled. Some thought they were drunk. Simon Peter who was one of Jesus' main disciples when He lived on earth was a leader and he spoke on behalf of the group. Peter told the crowd that they were witnessing prophecy being fulfilled. He referred to an Old Testament book named after a prophet called Joel. Joel said that what was being witnessed was a sign of the last days. (Time on earth has been divided up in dispensations - periods of time that are designated for specific activity.) This event that occurred after the ascension of Jesus into Heaven marked the beginning of the final dispensation called "the last days." We are moving toward the end of the world as we know it. The last book of the Bible, Revelation tells us what will happen after this dispensation ends. We will experience a new Heaven and earth that will have no problems and no end.

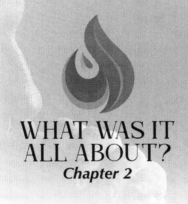

WHAT WAS IT ALL ABOUT?
Chapter 2

The purpose of the baptism with the Holy Spirit was to empower the Church to carry on the ministry of Jesus Christ. Jesus said in John 14:12 that His followers would do the same works He did after He returned to Heaven.

John 14:12 NKJV
"Most assuredly, I say to you, he who believes in Me, the works that I do he will

do also; and greater works than these he will do, because I go to My Father."

Luke 24:49 NJKV
Behold, I send the Promise of My Father upon you; but tarry in the city of Jerusalem until you are endued with power from on high."

Acts 1:8 NKJV
But you shall receive power when the Holy Spirit has come upon you; and you shall be witnesses to Me in Jerusalem, and in all Judea and Samaria, and to the end of the earth."

When we are born again, we are baptized by the Holy Spirit into the Body of Christ. So, we all have the Spirit in a measure.

1 Corinthians 12:13 NKJV
For by one Spirit we were all baptized into one body – whether Jew or Greeks, whether slaves or free – and have all been made to drink into one Spirit.

However, after the Holy Spirit baptizes us into the Body of Christ, Jesus baptizes us with the Holy Spirit.

Matthew 3:11 NKJV
I indeed baptize you with water unto repentance, but He who is coming after me is mightier than I, whose sandals I am not worthy to carry. He will baptize you with the Holy Spirit and fire.

HOW WE CAN
RECEIVE THIS GIFT
Chapter 3

There are different descriptions used
in the scriptures that refer to the same
experience. When we read "filled with the
Spirit," "baptized with the Holy Spirit," or
"receiving the gift of the Holy Spirit" the
same experience is being described.

**1. You must receive Jesus Christ as Savior
and Lord to qualify to receive this gift.
John 14:16-17 NLT**

And I will ask the Father, and he will give you another Advocate, who will never leave you. He is the Holy Spirit, who leads into all truth. The world cannot receive him, because it isn't looking for him and doesn't recognize him. But you know him, because he lives with you now and later will be in you.

Acts 2:38 NLT
Peter replied, "Each of you must repent of your sins and turn to God, and be baptized in the name of Jesus Christ for the forgiveness of your sins. Then you will receive the gift of the Holy Spirit.

Acts 8:14-17 NLT
When the apostles in Jerusalem heard that the people of Samaria had accepted God's message, they sent Peter and John there. As soon as they arrived, they prayed for these new believers to receive the Holy Spirit. The Holy Spirit had not yet come upon any of them, for they had only been

baptized in the name of the Lord Jesus. Then Peter and John laid their hands upon these believers, and they received the Holy Spirit.

2. You must ask for it.

Luke 11:9,13 NKJV

"So I say to you, ask, and it will be given to you; seek, and you will find; knock, and it will be opened to you.

If you then, being evil, know how to give good gifts to your children, how much more will your heavenly Father give the Holy Spirit to those who ask Him!"

This is a general statement as most people receive this way, although there are cases where people received without knowing about what they were receiving at the time. They were born again and wanting more from the Lord and had a supernatural encounter where they received the Holy Spirit and began speaking in a heavenly language. I received the Holy Spirit at age

10 years, about a year after being born again. I did not know much about it. I was being prayed for in an Assembly of God church. The person praying laid hands on me for something else other than the Holy Spirit, and I fell to the floor under the power of the Lord and began speaking in other tongues. The things of the Spirit were new to me. I had only heard the gospel for the first time at age 9 years, but I was eager to learn and experience more of the Lord.

In the scripture, there were people who received while listening to preaching. Obviously, they were receiving in their hearts as the representative of Jesus shared the gospel. (Acts 10:34-46) These people were baptized afterwards - showing that you can receive the Holy Spirit before being baptized in water. Therefore, it confirms that water baptism does not save you but is an act of obedience after you are saved. This incident also shows that you can receive the Holy Spirit immediately after you receive Christ as Savior and Lord.

3. You can receive by someone with experience putting their hands on you.

It is the spiritual law of contact and transmission. When contact is made, spiritual gifts are transmitted into the receiver.

Acts 8:14-17 NLT

When the apostles in Jerusalem heard that the people of Samaria had accepted God's message, they sent Peter and John there. As soon as they arrived, they prayed for these new believers to receive the Holy Spirit. The Holy Spirit had not yet come upon any of them, for they had only been baptized in the name of the Lord Jesus. Then Peter and John laid their hands upon these believers, and they received the Holy Spirit.

Acts 19:6 NKJV
And when Paul had laid hands on them,
the Holy Spirit came upon them, and they
spoke with tongues and prophesied.

BENEFITS OF BEING FILLED WITH THE HOLY SPIRIT
Chapter 4

When we receive the gift of the Holy Spirit, we are able to do supernatural works. 1 Corinthians 12:4-11 tells us about the kind of things we may be able to do to benefit others.

There are also personal benefits to being baptized with the Holy Spirit. The language the Holy Spirit gives us is a powerful prayer tool. It is called "praying with the spirit." We bypass our minds which is why we do not understand what we are saying.

1 Corinthians 14:14 NLT
For if I pray in tongues, my spirit is praying, but I don't understand what I am saying.

Romans 8:26-27 NLT
And the Holy Spirit helps us in our weakness. For example, we don't know what God wants us to pray for. But the Holy Spirit prays for us with groanings that cannot be expressed in words. [27] And the Father who knows all hearts knows what the Spirit is saying, for the Spirit pleads for us believers in harmony with God's own will.

According to the Bible, we can strengthen ourselves by praying in that language.

1 Corinthians 14:4a NLT
A person who speaks in tongues is
strengthened personally…

Jude 20 NKJV
But you, beloved, building yourselves
up on your most holy faith, praying
in the Holy Spirit

*We can praise and worship on a
higher level.*

Paul tells us we can pray with the spirit
anytime we want to. He said that he
prayed with the spirit and even sang
with the spirit. Then he also prayed and
sang with his understanding at will. So,
speaking in our Heavenly language can
be used in praise and worship. Paul says
we give thanks well in other tongues or
languages. (He said that if we are leading
in prayer, we should pray in our natural
language also so the people joining us can
understand and agree.)

1 Corinthians 14:15-17 NKJV

What is the conclusion then? I will pray with the spirit, and I will also pray with the understanding. I will sing with the spirit, and I will also sing with the understanding. Otherwise, if you bless with the spirit, how will he who occupies the place of the uninformed say "Amen" at the giving of thanks, since he does not understand what you say? For you indeed give thanks well, but the other is not edified.

Paul did it so often he believed he did it more than anyone in the church he was writing to.

1 Corinthians 14:18 NKJV

I thank my God I speak with tongues more than you all.

In 1 Corinthians 12 we read about two spiritual gifts called "different kinds of tongues and interpretation of tongues."

These are for use in ministry to others, not private prayer. 1 Corinthians 14 explains the difference. Paul tells us that we should not speak out loud in other tongues in a public setting unless there is an interpretation for everyone who is listening. Here he is talking about the spiritual gifts mentioned in chapter 12. In chapter 14, he talks about the private language where we are speaking to God, not men. The only time we can use our personal language out loud in a group setting is when it is a time of corporate prayer or worship and everyone is invited to pray or worship at the same time. In that case, nothing else will be taking place where we would be a distraction.

Another benefit of being filled with the Holy Spirit is it helps us experience the ministry He provides for believers in a greater way. Jesus said it was advantageous that He leave and send the Holy Spirit to the Church. If you ask them, most or all believers who have been filled with the Holy Spirit and practice praying in their Heavenly language will tell you it made a difference in them being able to know when the Lord was speaking to them or leading them.

John 16:7 NKJV
Nevertheless I tell you the truth. It is to your advantage that I go away; for if I do not go away, the Helper will not come to you; but if I depart, I will send Him to you.

In the gospel of John we read where Jesus told us that the Holy Spirit will be a helper, comforter, teacher, constant companion and guide. The Holy Spirit will receive instructions from the Father and Jesus and tell us about it. He will also tell us what's in the future. He will remind us of things Jesus told us in the Word or personally.
Note: *Certain words in the following verses were put in bold print for emphasis.*

John 14:16-18 NCV

I will ask the Father, and He will give you another **Helper**, to be with you forever— the Spirit of truth. The world cannot accept him, because it does not see him or know him. But you know Him, because he lives with you and he will be in you. I will not leave you all alone like orphans; I will come back to you.

John 14:16 in the KJV reads: "And I will pray the Father, and he shall give you another Comforter, that he may abide with you for ever;"

John 14:26 NKJV

But the Helper, the Holy Spirit, whom the Father will send in My name, He will teach you all things, and bring to your remembrance all things that I said to you.

John 16:13-15 NKJV

However, when He, the Spirit of truth, has come, He will guide you into all truth; for

He will not speak on His own authority, but whatever He hears He will speak; and He will tell you things to come. He will glorify Me, for He will take of what is Mine and declare it to you. All things that the Father has are Mine. Therefore I said that He will take of Mine and declare it to you.

HOW TO USE
WHAT WE HAVE
Chapter 5

Since we can activate the gift within us anytime we want to, we need to take advantage of the benefits. We should spend at least a few minutes in the morning praying with the spirit. Then we can try to increase the amount of time we pray this way throughout the day - getting dressed, driving, walking, etc. If we have difficulty falling asleep or

are awakened before we are supposed
to get up, we can pray with the spirit to
help us go to sleep and commune with
the Holy Spirit while we wait. It's better
than tossing and turning. We can use
it when trying to remember something
or find something. We can activate the
power when we are struggling spiritually
or trying to control emotions. We can
excuse ourselves and go to a private place
like the restroom for a moment if we need
to regroup and pray with the spirit.

Praying with the spirit is especially
helpful when we are not sure how to
pray about something. (See Romans 8:26-
27) The Holy Spirit knows exactly how
we need to pray and He will help us
pray in the perfect will of God. We may
understand what we are praying about
sometimes when we pray with our spirits,
but we don't have to. When we do not
understand, we trust God, believing what
the Bible says. We are praying in the will

of God and strengthening our spirits.

Another benefit of praying with the spirit is the devil does not understand and cannot interfere. The devil and people who are his agents hate praying with the spirit because they are unable to understand and interfere with our prayers. There are some things we should only pray about in the spirit.

THINGS THAT CAN HINDER US FROM RECEIVING THE HOLY SPIRIT OR HINDER US FROM PRAYING WITH THE SPIRIT

Chapter 6

Activity of evil spirits in our lives can hinder us from receiving or cause us to struggle with praying with the spirit after we receive. This is particularly true if we invite evil spirits knowingly or unknowingly. If we have not repented of sin, or have occult objects in our possession this could give the devil a way to hinder us spiritually. Once I had a gentleman come to me for prayer because he had difficulty praying with the spirit. I noticed he had a masonic ring on his finger. I asked if he was aware of the reasons he should not be associated with the lodge. He was not. After I explained it to him, he took off the ring and renounced his involvement with that organization. Then I prayed for him, and he fell under the power of the Lord and began to speak in other tongues fluently with no hindrance from that point on.

Sometimes, people are hindered because of prior teaching against the baptism with the Holy Spirit. They would need to study the scriptures to renew their minds and then submit their thinking to the Word of God. Others have challenges because they are so smart intellectually and have difficulty speaking in a language they do not understand. Those people need to humble themselves before the Lord and ask Him for help overcoming pride so they can receive. Proverbs 3:5 NLT says, "Trust in the LORD with all your heart; do not depend on your own understanding."

HOW TO INCREASE YOUR LANGUAGE IF YOU BEGIN WITH JUST A FEW SYLLABLES

Chapter 7

Sometimes people have received the gift of the Holy Spirit and seemingly are able to only say a few words which they repeat over and over. Be grateful for what you have received when you know it is not coming from your head but from your spirit. Also know that the

Holy Spirit has a language for you. The hindrance to speaking beyond those few words may be overcome with patience and concentration to connecting your spirit to the Holy Spirit. Place one hand on your belly and begin to speak in your heavenly language in slow motion. As more words come forth you can speed up slowly and you may be able to unclog the pipe, so to speak as you allow the Holy Spirit to give you more by focusing on Him more. Anxiousness to speak can cause you to stick with what you already know and hesitate to go beyond what you started with.

CONCLUSION

After we are born again, we qualify to receive the Holy Spirit. When we receive the Holy Spirit with the ability to speak in languages we did not learn, we should exercise that gift in prayer, praise and worship. We should also expect to be used to minister to others supernaturally as the Holy Spirit leads.

If you need help receiving or using the gift you received, talk to someone with experience who belongs to a church that believes in the gift of the Holy Spirit. I also recommend our 24-hour prayer line (More Than Conquerors Prayer Line) – 704-525-8638. I pray that this book will help and encourage you as well as enable you to help others.

ABOUT THE AUTHOR

A native of Nassau, Bahamas, Marilyn was born June 3, 1954 and born again at the age of  nine. She was filled with the Holy Spirit one year later. Like many baby Christians, Marilyn's zeal for the things of God without the knowledge of His word, resulted in many struggles. Her quest to have a deeper and stronger relationship with God brought her to Oral Roberts University, Tulsa, OK, where she subsequently met and married her late husband, Robyn Gool. Together they received the call of God to minister to the body of Christ. Marilyn stood in a supportive role alongside her husband who pastored Victory Christian Center in Charlotte, North Carolina from 1980 until he went to be with the Lord in November 2022. Fulfilling her late husband's desire and the will of the Lord, Marilyn took over the pastorate of VCC the same month after Robyn went to Heaven.

Pastor Marilyn Gool has taught the Word in the United States as well as many countries overseas. Her media exposure includes appearances on television locally and nationally. She has a radio program on Wordnet which airs weekdays at 12:30PM. The first week of each month she features a program called "The Value of Life in The Black Community." You can view past episodes of VLBC as a podcast on the church website, where you will also find a weekly short exhortation called "Light Snack." She has authored a four-part daily devotional entitled "Come Up Higher" and four mini-books entitled "How to Choose the Right Church," "How to Be a Good Church Member," "What to Do as a New Christian" and "Coming Home to Stay."

Other recommended books by Marilyn Gool:

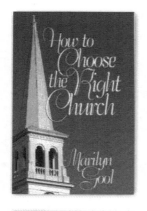

"How to Choose the Right Church"

ISBN #1-93027-257

"How to Be a Good Church Member"

ISBN #1-93027-265

Other recommended books by Marilyn Gool (continued):

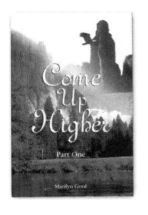

"Come Up Higher"
Devotional

Volume I - ISBN #0-9648460-2-0
Volume II - ISBN #0-9648460-3-9
Volume III - ISBN #0-9648460-4-7
Volume IV - ISBN #0-9648460-5-5

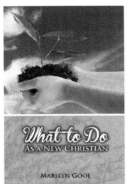

"What to Do As a New Christian"

ISBN #978-0-9798241-1-1

Other recommended books
by Marilyn Gool (continued):

**"Coming Home
to Stay"**

ISBN #978-0-9971292-1-2

Join Pastor Marilyn Gool for the *"Light Snack"* podcast!

Join Marilyn Gool for a "light snack" designed
to help you get understanding of God's Word at
vccenter.net/lightsnack, or you may also tune
in via the *VCC Charotte* mobile or TV apps,
or on the Facebook & Instagram pages.

"Lessons from the Word" Broadcast
Tune in to Dr. Gool's daily broadcast
"Lessons from the Word" Monday through Friday.
Check out the current broadcast
schedule on **wordnet.org**.

Have you visited the Throne Room lately?
**Visit the archived blog post at
vccenter.net/the-throne-room.**
Gain valuable insight into the Word and
receive encouragement beneficial
for a successful life."

Made in the USA
Columbia, SC
11 March 2024